D0274962

Deadly Dinosaurs

By Niki Foreman

LONDON, NEW YORK, MUNICH,
MELBOURNE, AND DELHI

DK LONDON
Series Editor Deborah Lock
Production Editor Francesca Wardell
Illustrator Jason Bays
Reading Consultant
Shirley Bickler

DK DELHI
Editor Nandini Gupta
Art Editor Shruti Soharia Singh
DTP Designer Anita Yadav
Picture Researcher Aditya Katyal
Dy. Managing Editor Soma B. Chowdhury
Design Consultant Shefali Upadhyay

First published in Great Britain by
Dorling Kindersley Limited
80 Strand, London, WC2R 0RL

Copyright © 2014 Dorling Kindersley Limited
A Penguin Company

10 9 8 7 6 5 4 3 2 1
001—195863—January/2014

A CIP catalogue record for this book is available from the British Library.

ISBN: 978-1-40934-726-2

Printed and bound in China by South China Printing Company.

The publisher would like to thank the following for their kind
permission to reproduce their photographs:
(Key: a-above; b-below/bottom; c-centre; f-far; l-left; r-right; t-top)
10 Dorling Kindersley: Dave King / Graham High at Centaur Studios - modelmaker (bl).
13 Dorling Kindersley: Jon Hughes / Bedrock Studios (br). **14 Dorling Kindersley:**
Natural History Museum, London (bl, cr, c). **15 Dorling Kindersley:** Andrew Kerr (br);
Natural History Museum, London (t) **16 Dorling Kindersley:** Jon Hughes (br).
18-19 The Natural History Museum, London: John Sibbick (c).
19 Science Photo Library: Natural History Museum, London (cr). **25 Dorling Kindersley:**
Andy Crawford (br). **27 Corbis:** ZUMA Press / La Daily News / Andy Holzman (tr).
30 Dorling Kindersley: Giuliano Fornari (bl). **31 Dorling Kindersley:** Andy Crawford /
Centaur Studios - modelmaker (cb); Natural History Museum, London (c, tr).
33 Dorling Kindersley: Jon Hughes (cr). **34-35 Dorling Kindersley:** Andrew Kerr (c).
42 Dorling Kindersley: Natural History Museum, London (cl, cb).
Pearson Asset Library: Coleman Yuen / Pearson Education Asia Ltd (bc, c);
Tudor Photography (tc). **43 Pearson Asset Library:** Coleman Yuen / Pearson Education
Asia Ltd (bc, tc). **44 Corbis:** ZUMA Press / La Daily News / Andy Holzman (bl).
45 Dreamstime.com: Marcio Silva
Jacket images: Front cover: Andrew Kerr **Spine:** Illustrator: Jason Bays
Back cover: (tr) Illustrator: Jason Bays, (l) Andy Crawford
All images © Dorling Kindersley

All other images © Dorling Kindersley

For further information see: www.dkimages.com

Discover more at
www.dk.com

Contents

The Museum at Night

It was night time
at the Dinosaur Museum.
No-one was around.

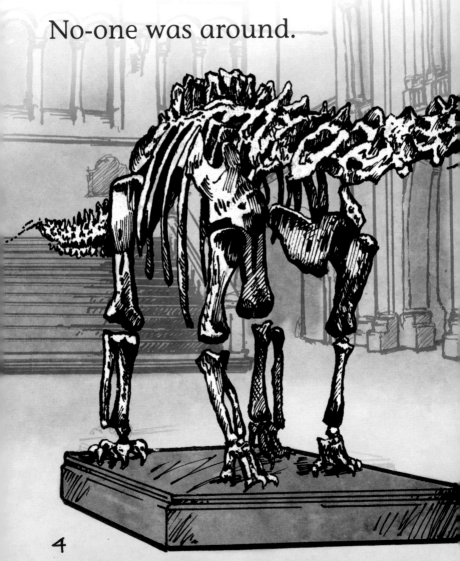

All was still and quiet,
but wait...

ROar!

What was that noise?

Thud!

The museum shook.
There was something
alive in the North Hall.

The Dinosaur Museum

ENTRANCE

Spinosaurus

WEST HALL

Tyrannosaurus
Rex

Sinornithosaurus

NORTH HALL

Deinonychus

SOUTH HALL

Chapter One

The North Hall was
full of fossils.

The fossils were the bones of
dead dinosaurs.

But there was something else
there, too –

something alive and hungry!

It stood up tall on two legs.

It had a long, stiff tail.

Swish!

Its teeth were sharp
like spikes.

It looked big and scary.

It was Rexy,
the *Tyrannosaurus Rex*.

Here is how to say
Tyrannosaurus Rex:
tie-RAN-oh-SOR-us-recks

ROAR!

The dinosaur models were alive!

Rexy was the best hunter
around.

His sight was sharp.

He was fast and strong.

His huge jaws could
bite into animals.

Crunch!

He could eat
an *Edmontosaurus* alive,
bones and all!

Here is how to say
Edmontosaurus:
ed-MON-toh-SOR-us

Terrifying Teeth

Snap! Bite! Dinosaurs ate different things so they had different types of teeth.

Knife-like bite

Megalosaurus was a meat eater. Its teeth were like knives: curved for stabbing and jagged for tearing. They kept growing and growing, then fell out and some more grew.

Megalosaurus's old and new teeth

A beaked *Triceratops* tooth

Scissor-like shredder

Triceratops was a plant eater. Its teeth had sharp edges like scissors. They would strip tough, spiky leaves and shred woody branches and tree trunks.

Chapter
Two

Rexy was hungry.

He was drooling.

Slop!

His drool dripped on
something small at his feet.

It was Sid, the *Sinornithosaurus*.

Here is how to say
Sinornithosaurus:
SIE-nor-ni-thoh-SOR-us

Sid was hungry, too.

RASSSSP!

Sinornithosaurus

This small dinosaur lived in China.
It lived around 125 million years ago.

Its teeth were like
the fangs of snakes.

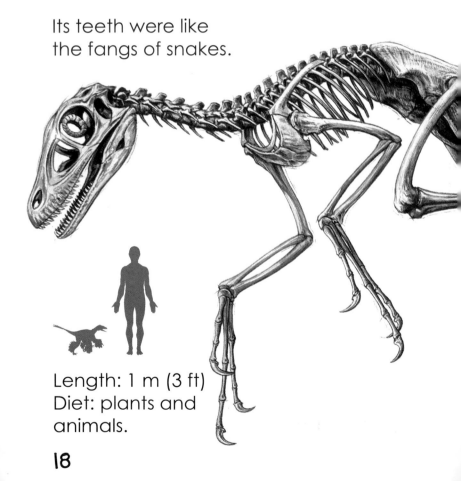

Length: 1 m (3 ft)
Diet: plants and
animals.

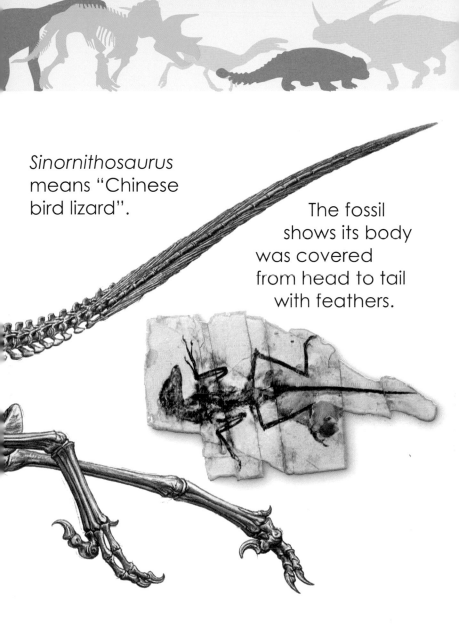

Sinornithosaurus means "Chinese bird lizard".

The fossil shows its body was covered from head to tail with feathers.

It could not fly, but scientists think it could climb trees.

Sid shook the drool off
his feathers.

His long, sharp teeth gleamed
in his beak.

Something moved.

Sid pounced.

He sunk his teeth into its flesh.

ROAR!

It was Rexy's foot!

Sid had a killer bite.
His teeth were loaded
with poison but
they were too small
to harm Rexy.
Sid gulped.
"Sorry, Rexy!"

Slop!

Another drip of drool
landed on him.

Chapter Three

Deano, the *Deinonychus*, pranced across the hall.

Thump!
Thump!

His long tail swept
from side to side.

Swish!

His two hooked claws tapped
on the floor.

Tap! Tap!

Here is how to say
Deinonychus:
die-NON-ee-kus

"You are such a featherbrain,
Sid!" drawled Deano.
"Biting old Rexy like that.
Tut tut.
Stick to your diet
of little dinosaurs.
Leave the big dinosaurs
to me!"

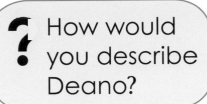
How would you describe Deano?

27

"You should see me hunt
with my friends.
We can kill a dinosaur
three times our size!
They call us the 'terrible claws'.
One slash from
these sharp claws and
dinner is ready."

Slash!

Deadly Claws

Stab! Slash! Dinosaurs used their claws to attack and defend.

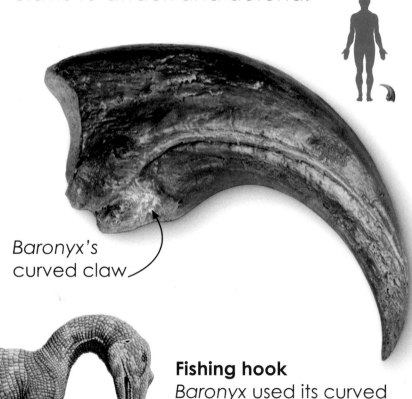

Baronyx's curved claw

Fishing hook
Baronyx used its curved claw like a harpoon to catch large fish for its dinner.

Iguanodon's spiked thumb

Useful claw

Iguanodon had a claw with many uses. Its thumb spike was for defending itself from meat eaters. Its three middle fingers were for walking on. Its fifth finger was for holding food.

31

"Did someone say 'dinner'?"
hissed Sonia, the *Spinosaurus*.

Her toothy snout sniffed for fish.
The sail on her back stood
tall and grand.
She was the biggest dinosaur.

Here is how to say
Spinosaurus:
SPY-no-SOR-us

Spinosaurus

This huge dinosaur lived in North Africa. It lived around 110 million years ago.

Spinosaurus means "spine lizard".

Length: 18 m (59 ft)
Diet: fish and other animals.

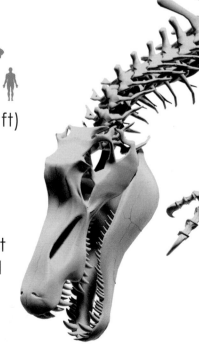

It was the biggest killer on land and it also hunted in water.

34

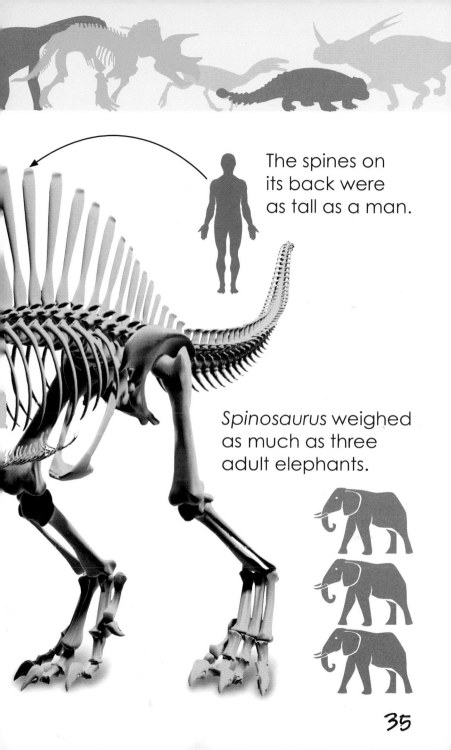

The spines on its back were as tall as a man.

Spinosaurus weighed as much as three adult elephants.

"I am the most deadly dinosaur," hissed Sonia.
"Oh no, you are not!" roared Rexy, Sid and Deano.

It is me!

"I am faster than Rexy," hissed Sonia.

"I have a more powerful bite than Sid.

I do not need help to kill like Deano.

I am the most deadly."

No, it is me!

It is me!

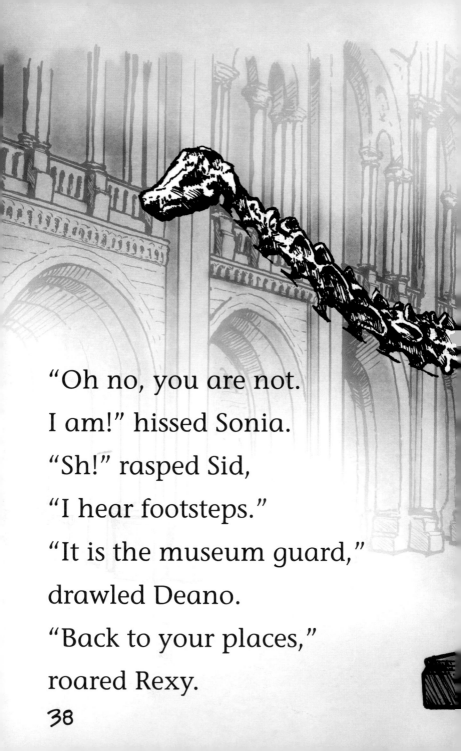

"Oh no, you are not.
I am!" hissed Sonia.
"Sh!" rasped Sid,
"I hear footsteps."
"It is the museum guard,"
drawled Deano.
"Back to your places,"
roared Rexy.
38

FREEZE!

All was still and quiet
in the North Hall.

39

Make a
Dinosaur Puppet

This colourful dinosaur puppet can nod its neck and wriggle its body. You will need: white card, coloured pens, varnish, cotton wool, a split pin, dowel sticks, two pins, a pair of scissors and a hammer.

1. Draw a big dinosaur on the white card. Mark its stripes. Colour it in bright colours.

40

2. Cut around your dinosaur. Cut the neck from its body.

3. Use cotton wool to dab varnish over the dinosaur. Let it dry.

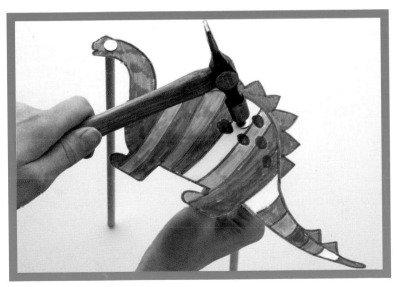

4. Ask an adult to connect the neck to its body with a split pin. Hammer a pin through to a dowel stick at its eye and on its back.

Dinosaur Game

Join Tibbs,
the Triceratops, for an adventure.

You will need: a counter for each player and a die.

To play: players take turns to throw the die and move the number of spaces shown.

START

Tibbs grazes with his herd.
MOVE ON 1 SPACE.

FINISH

Tibbs returns to his herd.
MOVE ON 1 SPACE.

Tibbs stabs with his horns.
MOVE ON 1 SPACE.

Rexy gives up the fight.
MOVE ON 1 SPACE.

Tibbs finds a tasty plant to eat. MISS A TURN.

Tibbs watches other dinosaurs. MOVE BACK 1 SPACE.

Rexy sees Tibbs. MOVE BACK 1 SPACE.

Tibbs turns to fight Rexy. MOVE ON 1 SPACE.

Tibbs kicks up dust. MOVE ON 1 SPACE.

Rexy roars! MOVE BACK 1 SPACE.

Dinosaur Quiz

1. What type of dinosaur is Rexy?

2. Which dinosaur was in the South Hall in the Dinosaur Museum?

3. What was Sid's body covered with?

4. Which meat-eating dinosaur was the biggest?

? Which dinosaur do you think was the deadliest?

Answers on page 48.

Glossary

attack fight another animal

defend try not to get
hurt in a fight

fossils remains of
animals and plants that
lived a long time ago

meat eater animal that eats
other animals

model copy of an object or
an animal

museum place where things
are put on display

plant eater animal
that eats
parts of plants

Guide for Parents

DK Reads is a three-level interactive reading adventure series for children, developing the habit of reading widely for both pleasure and information. These chapter books have an exciting main narrative interspersed with a range of reading genres to suit your child's reading ability, as required by the National Curriculum. Each book is designed to develop your child's reading skills, fluency, grammar awareness, and comprehension in order to build confidence and engagement when reading.

Ready for a *Beginning to Read* book

YOUR CHILD SHOULD

- be using phonics, including consonant blends, such as bl, gl and sm, to read unfamiliar words; and common word endings, such as plurals, ing, ed and ly.

- be using the storyline, illustrations and the grammar of a sentence to check and correct his/her own reading.

- be pausing briefly at commas, and for longer at full stops; and altering his/her expression to respond to question, exclamation and speech marks.

A VALUABLE AND SHARED READING EXPERIENCE

For many children, reading requires much effort but adult participation can make this both fun and easier. So here are a few tips on how to use this book with your child.

TIP 1 Check out the contents together before your child begins:

- read the text about the book on the back cover.

- read through and discuss the contents page together to heighten your child's interest and expectation.

- make use of unfamiliar or difficult words on the page in a brief discussion.

- chat about the non-fiction reading features used in the book, such as headings, captions, recipes, lists or charts.

TIP 2 Support your child as he/she reads the story pages:

- give the book to your child to read and turn the pages.
- where necessary, encourage your child to break a word into syllables, sound out each one and then flow the syllables together. Ask him/her to reread the sentence to check the meaning.
- when there's a question mark or an exclamation mark, encourage your child to vary his/her voice as he/she reads the sentence. Demonstrate how to do this if it is helpful.

TIP 3 Praise, share and chat:

- the factual pages tend to be more difficult than the story pages, and are designed to be shared with your child.
- ask questions about the text and the meaning of the words used. These help to develop comprehension skills and awareness of the language used.

A FEW ADDITIONAL TIPS

- Try and read together everyday. Little and often is best. These books are divided into manageable chapters for one reading session. However after 10 minutes, only keep going if your child wants to read on.
- Always encourage your child to have a go at reading difficult words by themselves. Praise any self-corrections, for example, "I like the way you sounded out that word and then changed the way you said it, to make sense."
- Read other books of different types to your child just for enjoyment and information.

Series consultant **Shirley Bickler** is a longtime advocate of carefully crafted, enthralling texts for young readers. Her LIFT initiative for infant teaching was the model for the National Literacy Strategy Literacy Hour, and she is co-author of *Book Bands for Guided Reading* published by Reading Recovery based at the Institute of Education.

Index

Answers to the Dinosaur Quiz:
1. *Tyrannosaurus Rex*; **2.** Deano,
the *Deinonychus*; **3.** Feathers; **4.** *Spinosaurus*.